# Instant Pot Mini

## Learn How to Master Your Instant Pot Mini

*Must-Have, Easy and Healthy Instant Pot Recipes that Put Your Pressure Cooker to Work*

**ISBN:**9781090429872
Liam Sandler© 2019

# Table of Contents

# Introduction

The instant pot mini is perfect for someone who cooks for just themselves, themselves and a significant other or themselves and a small family. There's no reason to get a big instant pot, and there's no reason to avoid one and instead slave away in the kitchen either. You can have the advantage of an instant pot without the bulk. The instant pot has become a kitchen necessity since it can take the place of seven main kitchen appliances. There's no reason to slave away in the kitchen for healthy, delicious food made easy.

# Getting Started

You may be wondering why you want to choose the instant pot when cooking. It's just a smaller version of the original instant pot. It will do the same thing as seven different kitchen appliances. It can be a sauté pan, yogurt maker, food warmer, steamer, slow cooker, rice cooker and pressure cooker, which makes your time in the kitchen even easier. If an instant pot is too big for you, then the miniature is perfect! The best part is that it's perfect travel size, so you can even use it on an RV or boat! You may think that it's too small for your needs, but keep in mind that it can cook up to six cups of rice. The dimensions are usually 7.8 by 5 inches.

## What It comes With

Your instant pot mini will come with a lot of accessories. You'll find them below.

- Steamer Rack (Stainless Steel without Handles)
- Soup Spoon
- Rice Paddle
- Measuring Cup (for Rice)
- Inner Cooking Pot
- Condensation Collector
- Steamer Rack (Stainless Steel)
- Detachable Power Cord
- User Manual
- Recipe Booklet
- Reference Guide

# Buttons & Features

There are elven "Smart Programmable" controls that are already included in your instant pot mini. They are as followed:

- Keep Warm
- Yogurt
- Porridge
- Meat/Stew
- Bean/Chili
- Soup/Broth
- Slow Cook
- Pressure Cook (Manual)
- Steam
- Sauté
- Rice

Furthermore, you can adjust three programs with three different settings. These settings are "less", "normal" or "more".

When you use the sauté button as well as the slow cook button you can choose from high, normal and low temperature. You can also set a twenty-four hour delay that will allow you to postpone cooing until you're ready for dinner. It will automatically switch to "keep warm" which retains the heat until you're ready to serve the food too. There's no reason to worry about ever serving your food cold

# DIFFERENT METHODS OF COOKING

Let's take a deeper look at the cooking methods that you can use with the instant pot mini.

- **Steam:** this is the process of cooking food by using boiling water which turns into steam when it vaporizes. The hat is then carried to the food by placing it over that water. Your food does not come into contact with the water when you steam it, which allows for nutrient preservation and a more intense flavor.

- **Slow Cook:** With this method you simmer the food with low heat for longer periods which will soften meat and vegetables.

- **Sauté:** With this cooking method you cook food with a small amount of fat or oil using high heat. It's beat for searing vegetables and browning meat. It can also be used to boil, simmer and reduce liquid.

# Breakfast Recipes

## Strawberry Oatmeal

**Serves:** 3 **Time:** 25 Minutes

**Calories:** 246 **Protein:** 6.3 Grams

**Fat:** 10.3 Grams **Carbs:** 37.4 Grams

**Ingredients:**

- 1 Tablespoon Butter
- 1 Cup Steel Cut Oats
- 1 ½ Cups Strawberries, Fresh & Sliced
- ¼ Cup Cream
- 3 Tablespoons Brown Sugar
- 4 Tablespoons Chia Seeds
- ¼ Teaspoon Sea Salt, Fine
- 4 Cups Water

**Directions:**

1. Start by adding your butter into your instant pot mini and then press sauté.
2. Once it's melted, you'll cook your oats for three minutes while stirring constantly.
3. Add in your brown sugar, cream, salt and water. Stir well and then seal the instant pot mini. Cook on high pressure for ten minutes.
4. Use a natural pressure release, and then add in your strawberries and chia seeds. Make sure that you stir well before serving.

# Mushroom Omelet

**Serves:** 4 **Time:** 15 Minutes

**Calories:** 229 **Protein:** 9.4 Grams

**Fat:** 18.9 Grams

**Carbs:** 7.8 Grams

**Ingredients:**

- 5 Eggs, Beaten Lightly
- 2 Tablespoon Chives, Minced
- ½ Cup Coconut Milk
- 1 ½ Cups Mushrooms, Sliced
- ½ Tablespoon Cheddar Cheese
- 1 Onion, Chopped
- 1 Bell Pepper, Chopped

**Directions:**

1. Start by adding in your butter and then heat it up by pressing sauté. Get out a bowl and beat your eggs.

2. Add your ingredients into the instant pot, pouring your egg mixture in last. Cook for two minutes using sauté.

3. Seal your pot, cooking on high pressure for eight minutes. Release the pressure with a quick release and serve hot.

# CHERRY & CINNAMON RISOTTO

**Serves:** 2 **Time:** 25 Minutes

**Calories:** 423 **Protein:** 11 Grams

**Fat:** 3 Grams

**Carbs:** 29 Grams

**Ingredients:**

- ¼ Cup Brown Sugar
- ¼ Cup Cherries, Dried
- 1 Tablespoon Butter
- ¾ Cup Arborio Rice
- ½ Cup Apple Juice
- 1 Apple, Large, Peeled, Cored & Diced
- ¾ Teaspoon Cinnamon
- 1 ½ Cups Milk
- Almond Flakes for Garnish

**Directions:**

1. Start by adding your butter into your instant pot mini with your rice, and press sauté so you can cook it for three to four minutes. It should become translucent and soften. Add in your sugar, spices, and apple. Stir gently.

2. Add in your juice and milk. Mix to combine well, and then lock the instant potlid. Cook on high pressure for six minutes. Use a quick release, and then serve warm. Make sure you top with cherries and almonds.

# ITALIAN SAUSAGE BREAKFAST

**Serves:** 3

**Time:** 30 Minutes

**Calories:** 376

**Protein:** 23 Grams

**Fat:** 9 Grams

**Carbs:** 8 Grams

**Ingredients:**

- ½ Tablespoon Basil, Dried
- 7 Ounces Tomato Sauce
- ½ Cup Water
- 4 Italian Sausages
- 14 Ounces Tomatoes, Canned & Diced
- 2 Green Bell Peppers, Sliced into Strips
- ½ Tablespoon Italian Seasoning
- 1 Teaspoon Garlic, Minced

**Directions:**

1. Get out a baking dish that will fit into your instant pot, and then grease it. Throw in all of your ingredients, and make sure to combine it well.
2. Pour the water into the bottom of your instant pot mini before placing in your trivet. Put your baking dish on top of your trivet and then lock the lid.
3. Cook on high pressure for twenty-five minutes, and then use a quick release.
4. Serve warm.

# BUCKWHEAT & FRUIT PORRIDGE

**Serves:** 2

**Time:** 15 Minutes

**Calories:** 163

**Protein:** 5 Grams

**Fat:** 0 Grams

**Carbs:** 13 Grams

**Ingredients:**

- 3 Cups Milk
- 1 Cup Buckwheat, Rinsed
- 1 Banana, Sliced
- ½ Teaspoon Vanilla Extract, Pure
- ½ Cup Raisins

**Directions:**

1. Combine all of your ingredients into your instant pot, and then stir to make sure it's combined.

2. Cook on high pressure for six minutes, and then use a natural pressure release. Serve warm.

# CHEESY HAM CASSEROLE

**Serves:** 2

**Time:** 35 Minutes

**Calories:** 208

**Protein:** 7 Grams

**Fat:** 6 Grams

**Carbs:** 5 Grams

**Ingredients:**

- 1 Cup Ham, Chopped
- 6 Eggs
- 4 Red Potatoes, Cubed
- 1 Cup Cheddar Cheese, Shredded
- ½ Yellow Onion, Chopped
- 1 Cup Milk
- 2 Cups Water
- Pinch Sea Salt & Water

**Directions:**

1. Get out a mixing bowl and whisk your mil, pepper, salt, potatoes, eggs, ham, onion and cheese. Make sure it's well combined.

2. Take a baking pan that fits in your instant pot mini and grease it with cooking spray. Pour in your cheese mix, and then pour your water into your instant pot mini. Add in your trivet with your pan on top. Lock the lid, and cook for twenty-five minutes on high pressure.

3. Use a natural release, and then serve warm.

# PEACH QUINOA TREAT

**Serves:** 2 **Time:** 15 Minutes

**Calories:** 364 **Protein:** 13 Grams

**Fat:** 3 Grams

**Carbs:** 47 Grams

**Ingredients:**

- ½ Cup Water
- ½ Teaspoon Vanilla Extract, Pure
- 1 Cup Peaches
- 1 Tablespoon Cinnamon
- 1 Cup Quinoa, Rinsed & Drained
- ¾ Cup Half & Half
- ½ Cup Water
- 1 Tablespoon Butter
- 1 Cup Milk

**Directions:**

1. Press sauté on your instant pot mini and add in your quinoa and butter. Stir well and cook for two minutes. Your quinoa should become softer. Dd in your water and milk, and stir gently.
2. Add in your cinnamon and vanilla, making sure it's mixed well.
3. Lock your lid before cooking on high pressure for four minutes.
4. Use a quick release, and mix in your half and half as well as your peaches.
5. Serve immediately.

# CHEESY BREAKFAST POTATOES

**Serves:** 2

**Time:** 20 Minutes

**Calories:** 254

**Protein:** 12 Grams

**Fat:** 12 Grams

**Carbs:** 13 Grams

**Ingredients:**

- 1 Teaspoon Parsley, Dried
- Sea Salt & Black Pepper to Taste
- ½ lb. Red Potatoes, Cubed
- ½ Teaspoon Garlic Powder
- 1 Bacon Strip, Chopped
- 1 Ounce Ranch Dressing
- 1 Tablespoon Water
- 1 ½ Ounces Cheddar Cheese, Grated

**Directions:**

1. Open your lid and add in all of your ingredients except for your cheese and dressing. Stir to combine it well, and then cook on high pressure for seven minutes.

2. Use a natural pressure release, and then mix in your dressing and cheese before serving warm.

# APPLE CINNAMON PORRIDGE

**Serves:** 2 **Time:** 30 Minutes

**Calories:** 312 **Protein:** 13.5 Grams

**Fat:** 0.8 Grams

**Carbs:** 44 Grams

**Ingredients:**

- 1 ¼ lb. Whole squash
- 2 Apples, Cored & Chopped
- 1/8 Teaspoon Ginger
- 1/8 Teaspoon Cloves
- ½ Teaspoon Cinnamon
- ½ Cup Chicken Broth
- 2 Tablespoons Maple syrup
- 2 Tablespoon Gelatin
- Pinch Sea Salt, Fine

**Directions:**

1. Place your broth, spices, apples and squash in your instant pot mini. Stir your ingredients, and then cook on high pressure for eight minutes. Allow it to have a natural pressure release, and then take the squash out.

2. Place your squash on a cutting board and half it lengthwise. Make sure to discard the seeds.

3. Get out a blender and add in your squash flesh, apple mixture, maple syrup, gelatin and salt. Pulse until it's smooth before serving.

# EGG & BACON DELIGHT

**Serves:** 2

**Time:** 15 Minutes

**Calories:** 286

**Protein:** 16 Grams

**Fat:** 6 Grams

**Carbs:** 5 Grams

**Ingredients:**

- 2 Ounces Bacon, Chopped
- 4 Eggs
- ½ Teaspoon Sea Salt, Fine
- 1 Teaspoon Basil, Chopped
- ½ Teaspoon Paprika
- Black Pepper to Taste

**Directions:**

1. whisk your eggs with basil, spices and cilantro.
2. Press sauté, and then add in your bacon. Cook while stirring for three minutes before adding in your egg mix. Cook four about five minutes. Scramble your eggs, and then transfer to a plate to serve warm.

# CRUST FREE QUICHE

**Serves:** 2

**Time:** 40 Minutes

**Calories:** 212

**Protein:** 8 Grams

**Fat:** 3 Grams

**Carbs:** 7 Grams

**Ingredients:**

- 1 Cup Water
- 3 Eggs
- ½ Cup Cheddar Cheese, Shredded
- 1 Tablespoon Chives, Chopped
- ¼ Cup Milk
- Sea Salt & Black Pepper to Taste

**Directions:**

1. Whisk your salt, chives, pepper, milk and eggs together before getting out a baking pan that will fit in your instant pot mini. Grease it down using cooking spray. Add your cheese in, and then top with your egg mixture.

2. Cover your pan using foil, and pour the water into your instant pot mini. Put your trivet on top, and put the pan on the trivet. Lock your lid and cook for thirty minutes on high pressure.

3. Allow for a natural pressure release and then serve warm.

# Breakfast Frittatas

**Serves:** 3

**Time:** 15 Minutes

**Calories:** 288

**Protein:** 13.9 Grams

**Fat:** 17.7 Grams

**Carbs:** 4.5 Grams

**Ingredients:**

- 1 Scallion, Chopped
- 1 Zucchini, Chopped
- 4 Tablespoons Cheddar Cheese, Shredded
- 2 Bacon Slices, Cooked
- ¼ Teaspoons Lemon Pepper Seasoning
- 3 Eggs
- ¼ Cup Almond Milk
- Sea Salt & Black Pepper to Taste

**Directions:**

1. Pour your water into your instant pot. It should be about a cup and then put your trivet on top. Toss all of your ingredients in a bowl, whisking well so that it's combined.

2. Pour your mixture into silicone molds, and then seal on high pressure for five minutes.

3. Use a quick release, and serve warm.

# PISTACHIO QUINOA

**Serves:** 2 **Time:** 15 Minutes

**Calories:** 418 **Protein:** 14 Grams

**Fat:** 6.5 Grams **Carbs:** 44.5 Grams

**Ingredients:**

- 1/8 Cup Raisins
- ¾ Cup White Quinoa
- 1/8 Cup Pistachios, Chopped
- ½ Cup Apple Juice
- 3 Tablespoons Blueberries
- ½ Cup Plain Yogurt
- ½ Cup Apples, Grated / ½ Tablespoon Honey, Raw
- 1 Cinnamon Stick, Small  / ¾ Cup Water

**Directions:**

1. Rinse your quinoa through a fine mesh strainer, and then add your water, cinnamon stick and quinoa to your instant pot mini.

2. Cook on high pressure for one minute, and then use a natural pressure release. It should take about ten minutes.

3. Spoon your quinoa into a bowl and then mix in apple, apple juice, raisins, honey and remove your cinnamon stick.

4. Keep it in the fridge for at least an hour, and then add in your yogurt. Stir well, topping with blueberries and pistachios before serving.

# POTATO RICE

**Serves:** 3 **Time:** 20 Minutes

**Calories:** 377 **Protein:** 13.7 Grams

**Fat:** 12 Grams **Carbs:** 55.6 Grams

**Ingredients:**

- 2 Lean Sausages, Sliced Thin
- 4 Slices Ginger
- 1 ½ Tablespoons Green Onion, Chopped Fine
- 5 Yellow Potatoes', Small & Peeled
- 1 ½ Tablespoons Olive Oil
- Pinch Black Pepper \ 2 Cups Long Grain Rice
- 1 Tablespoon Green Onion, Chopped Fine
- ¼ Cup Chicken Broth
- 3 Cups Water \1 Teaspoon Sea Salt, Fine

**Directions:**

1. Press sauté and add in your onions, ginger and oil. Cook for two minutes. Your ingredients should begin to soften.

2. Add the sausages and cook for about two minutes. Add in your potatoes, and then cook for another two minutes. Add in your rice, stirring well to combine.

3. Add in all of the rest of your ingredients, and then seal your instant pot mini.

4. Press the rice button and then set the time for four minutes.

5. Allow for a natural pressure release which will take about ten minutes.

6. Garnish with green onions before serving.

# Mango Rice

**Serves:** 3

**Time:** 15 Minutes

**Calories:** 261

**Protein:** 4 Grams

**Fat:** 6 Grams

**Carbs:** 38.4 Grams

**Ingredients:**

- 1 Cup Mango Chunks
- 2 Tablespoons Brown Sugar
- Black Sesame Seeds as Needed
- 1 ¼ Cup Coconut Milk, Sweetened Lightly
- 1 Cup White Jasmine Rice, Uncooked
- 1/3 Cup Coconut Milk, Lightly Sweetened

**Directions:**

1. Start placing 1 ¼ cups coconut milk, rice and mango in the pot, and then lock the lid. Cook for four minutes on high pressure, and then allow for a natural pressure release which will take roughly ten minutes.

2. Mix in your remaining coconut milk and top with brown sugar and black sesame seeds as desired.

# Sweet Potato Hash

**Serves:** 2 **Time:** 20 Minutes

**Calories:** 256 **Protein:** 4 Grams

**Fat:** 12 Grams

**Carbs:** 21.5 Grams

**Ingredients:**

- 1 Cup Bell Pepper, Chopped
- ½ Teaspoon Pepper
- 1 Potato, Diced
- 1 Teaspoon Cumin
- 1 Clove Garlic, Minced
- 1 Teaspoon Paprika
- 1 Tablespoon Oil
- 1 Sweet Potato, Diced
- ¼ Cup Water
- ½ Teaspoon Sea Salt, Fine
- Pinch Cayenne

**Directions:**

1. Toss your potatoes and pepper with your spices and oil. Place them in your instant pot, and add in a half a cup of water. Close the pot, and then cook on high pressure for ten minutes.

2. Use a quick release, and then press sauté. Brown your potatoes before serving warm.

# Lunch Recipes

## CHEESY PORK MACARONI

**Serves:** 2 **Time:** 25 Minutes

**Calories:** 368 **Protein:** 19.2 Grams

**Fat:** 30.7 Grams

**Carbs:** 3.8 Grams

**Ingredients:**

- ¼ lb. Ground Pork
- ¼ Cup Cheddar, Grated
- ¼ Cup Macaroni, Cooked
- 1 Tablespoon Olive Oil
- 2 Eggs
- 2 Tablespoons Mushroom, Diced
- ½ Teaspoon Pepper 2 Teaspoons Garlic Powder

**Directions:**

1. Start by combining all of your ingredients except for your cheese in a bowl. Transfer the mixture to an aluminum pan, and make sure it's spread out.

2. Sprinkle your cheese on top and pour in your water. Place your trivet in and then put your pan on top.

3. Seal your instant pot and cook on high pressure for twenty minutes.

4. Use a natural pressure release, and then serve warm.

# PORK TACO BOWL

**Serves:** 8

**Time:** 1 Hour 10 Minutes

**Calories:** 295

**Protein:** 32.6 Grams

**Fat:** 14.3 Grams

**Carbs:** 6.1 Grams

**Ingredients:**

- 2 Teaspoons Cumin Powder
- 2 Teaspoon Garlic Powder
- 2 Teaspoons Sea Salt, Fine
- 2 Teaspoons Black Pepper
- 2 Tablespoons Olive Oil
- 20 Ounces Green Chili Tomatillo Salsa
- 2 lb. Pork Sirloin Roast, Sliced Thick

**Directions:**

1. Place the garlic powder, salt, pepper, and ground cumin together in a bowl. Make sure it's mixed well, and then put your pork in a bowl, dredging it through the mixture.

2. Add your oil to your instant pot and press sauté. Once the pork is browned, secure the lid and cook for forty-five minutes on high pressure.

3. Allow for a natural pressure release before serving warm.

# CHEESY BEEF ROLL

**Serves:** 2 **Time:** 25 Minute

**Calories:** 387 **Protein:** 22.1 Grams

**Fat:** 29.9 Grams **Carbs:** 6.6 Grams

**Ingredients:**

- ¾ lbs. Ground Beef
- 2 Tablespoons Onion, Diced
- 2 Tablespoons Milk, Fresh
- 2 Tablespoons Flour
- ¾ Teaspoon Worcestershire Sauce \ 1 Egg White
- ¼ Cup Mozzarella Cheese, Grated
- 2 Tablespoons Ketchup
- Sea Salt & Black Pepper to Taste

**Directions:**

1. Start by mixing your egg white and ground beef together, and then add in your milk, flour, salt, pepper, onion, ketchup and Worcestershire to a bowl. Make sure it's mixed well, and roll the mixture. Wrap with foil and make sure to bind it tightly.

2. Pour your water into the instant pot and then add in your trivet. Place the roll on the trivet, and then seal your lid.

3. Cook on high pressure for eighteen minutes.

4. Allow for a natural pressure release, and allow it to cool before unwrapping it to slice.

5. Serve warm.

# Beef & Cheese Casserole

**Serves:** 4

**Time:** 20 Minutes

**Calories:** 749

**Protein:** 63 Grams

**Fat:** 28.3 Grams

**Carbs:** 38 Grams

## Ingredients:

- 2 Cups Beef Broth
- ½ Cup Cottage Cheese
- 1 Teaspoon Olive Oil
- ½ Green Bell Pepper, Seeded & Sliced
- ½ Cup Cheddar Cheese, Grated
- ½ Box Shell Pasta
- 1 Onion, Chopped
- 3 Ounce Package Cream Cheese, Softened
- 1 lb. Ground Beef, Lean
- 7.5 Ounces Tomatoes, Canned & Diced
- 7.5 Ounces Tomato Sauce
- Sea Salt & Black Pepper to Taste

**Directions:**

1. Add in your oil and press sauté. Once it's hot add in your onion and cook for two minutes so that it softens.

2. Add your beef in and cook for another four minutes. It should no longer be pink, and then season with slat and pepper.

3. Add in your tomato sauce and diced tomatoes. Throw in your cottage cheese cream cheese and bell peppers. Mix well, and then add in your beef broth and pasta. There should be enough liquid to cover the pasta. If not, then just add more. Close the lid and cook on high pressure for five minutes.

4. Use a quick release, and then add your cheddar cheese. Stir until melted, and serve warm.

# LETTUCE PORK WRAPS

**Serves:** 6 **Time:** 1 Hour 5 Minutes

**Calories:** 514 **Protein:** 39.2 Grams

**Fat:** 35.5 Grams **Carbs:** 7.6 Grams

**Ingredients:**

- 3 lb. Pork Shoulder, Bone In
- ½ Teaspoon Oregano
- 1 ¼ Onion, Chopped
- ½ Teaspoon Cayenne
- 1 ¼ Tablespoon Olive Oil
- 1 ¼ Oranges / 6 Lettuce Leaves
- ¾ Teaspoon Garlic Powder
- ¾ Teaspoon Cumin
- ½ Teaspoon Black Pepper / ¾ Teaspoon Sea Salt

**Directions:**

1. Throw all of your ingredients except for your lettuce in with your pork, and allow it to marinate overnight.
2. Heat your oil up and then press sauté.
3. Cook your pork in the oil, searing for ten minutes.
4. Add in two cups of water, and cook on medium pressure for forty-five minutes
5. Allow for a natural pressure release, and then shred.
6. Serve on lettuce leaves.

# PEPPER SALAD

**Serves:** 3

**Time:** 25 Minutes

**Calories:** 186

**Protein:** 11 Grams

**Fat:** 1 Gram

**Carbs:** 24 Grams

**Ingredients:**

- ½ Red Bell Pepper, Chopped
- 1 Teaspoon Dijon Mustard
- 15 Ounces Cannellini Beans, Canned & Rinsed
- 1 Tablespoon Olive Oil
- 1 Teaspoon Thyme, Fresh
- ¼ Onion, Small & Sliced
- 1 Tablespoon Vinegar
- Sea Salt & Black Pepper to Taste

**Directions:**

1. Start by adding your water and beans. Season with salt and pepper, and then lock the lid.
2. Cook on high pressure for twenty minutes, and then allow for a natural pressure release.
3. Mix in your remaining ingredients and serve warm.

# SPINACH & CHICKPEA CURRY

**Serves:** 3 **Time:** 25 Minutes

**Calories:** 452 **Protein:** 53 Grams

**Fat:** 4 Gram **Carbs:** 27 Grams

**Ingredients:**

- ½ Cup Vegetable Stock
- 3 Tablespoons Red Curry Paste
- ½ Tablespoon Sea Salt, Fine
- ½ Tablespoon Turmeric
- 1 Onion, Diced
- 8 Ounces White Mushrooms, sliced
- ¾ Cup Chickpeas
- 1 Tablespoon Ginger
- 2 Cloves Garlic, Minced
- 1 Green Chili, Seeded & Diced
- 1 Can Coconut Milk
- 1 Teaspoon Cumin
- ¼ Teaspoon Black Pepper
- 1 Tablespoon Tomato Paste
- ½ Teaspoon Curry powder
- ¼ Teaspoon Fenugreek
- 2 Teaspoons Lemon Juice, Fresh
- 1 Cup Spinach

- Olive Oil as Needed

**Directions:**

1. Start by saluting your onion and mushrooms until they soften. It will take about two minutes.

2. Add in your turmeric, ginger, garlic and chili. Cook for about two minutes more. Add in your remaining ingredients except for your lemon juice, spinach and tomato paste. Lock the lid, and cook on high pressure for fifteen minutes.

3. Use a quick release, and then mix in your lemon juice, spinach and tomato paste. Serve warm.

# MUSHROOM CURRY

**Serves:** 2

**Time:** 10 Minutes

**Calories:** 461

**Protein:** 37 Grams

**Fat:** 2 Grams

**Carbs:** 61 Grams

**Ingredients:**

- ½ Cup Vegetable Stock, Low Sodium
- ¼ Cup Red Wine
- 2 Teaspoons Soy Sauce
- 16 Ounces Mushrooms
- 6 Cloves Garlic, Peeled & Crushed
- 1 Tablespoon Browning Sauce
- Black Pepper to Taste

**Directions:**

1. Start by opening the lid and then add in all of your ingredients. Stir to combine before locking the lid.
2. Cook on high pressure for four minutes, and then use a quick release. Serve warm.

# Spinach & Eggplant Chili

**Serves:** 2

**Time:** 12 Minutes

**Calories:** 114

**Protein:** 3 Grams

**Fat:** 1 Grams

**Carbs:** 8 Grams

**Ingredients:**

- ½ Teaspoon Chili Powder
- 1 Cup Spinach, Torn
- 1 Tablespoon Coconut Oil
- ½ Cup Vegetable Stock
- ¼ Cup Coconut Milk
- 2 Cups Eggplant, cubed
- ½ Tablespoon Five Spice Powder

**Directions:**

1. Press sauté and then add in your eggplant cubes along with you oil. Cook for two minutes so that your eggplant cubes soften. Then you can add in your stock and coconut milk. Stir well.

2. Add in your seasonings and spinach, and then lock the instant pot mini's lid. Cook for four minutes on high pressure.

3. Use a quick release, and then serve warm.

# BACON BRUSSEL SPROUTS

**Serves:** 3

**Time:** 15 Minutes

**Calories:** 218

**Protein:** 16 Grams

**Fat:** 1 Grams

**Carbs:** 16 Grams

**Ingredients:**

- ¼ Cup Soy Sauce
- 4 Bacon Slices, Chopped
- 1 lb. Brussel Sprouts, Trimmed & Halved
- ¼ Cup Apple Cider Vinegar
- Sea Salt & Black Pepper to Taste

**Directions:**

1. Press and then add in your bacon. Cook for four to five minutes before adding in all of your remaining ingredients.
2. Lock the lid, and cook on high pressure for four minutes.
3. Use a quick release and serve warm.

# Dinner Recipes

## Spinach & Rosemary Salmon

**Serves:** 2

**Time:** 25 Minutes

**Calories:** 423

**Protein:** 41 Grams

**Fat:** 8 Grams

**Carbs:** 15 Grams

**Ingredients:**

- 1/2 Tablespoon Lemon Juice
- ½ Tablespoon Rosemary, Chopped
- 1 Cup Water
- ½ lb. Spinach, Torn
- ½ lb. Salmon Fillet, boneless
- ½ Clove Garlic, Chopped Fine
- 1 ½ Tablespoons Olive Oil
- Sea Salt & Black Pepper to Taste

**Directions:**

1. Start by cooking your spinach in a deep saucepan and cover jus enough water for it to wilt. Drain it and set it to the side.

2. Press sauté, and then add in your oil, salt, rosemary, pepper and salmon. Cook for three minutes, and stir together.

3. Add in your lemon juice along with ½ cup of water. Stir so that it's combined.

4. Lock your lid, and cook on high pressure for four minutes.

5. Use a quick release, and then add in ½ cup of water, spinach and garlic. Press sauté, and then cook for eight minutes. The sauce should thicken.

6. Serve topped with spinach sauce.

# CHEDDAR HADDOCK

**Serves:** 2

**Time:** 15 Minutes

**Calories:** 196

**Protein:** 18 Grams

**Fat:** 6 Grams

**Carbs:** 7 Grams

**Ingredients:**

- ½ Teaspoon Ginger
- 2 Ounces Cheddar Cheese, Grated
- Sea Salt & Black Pepper to Taste
- 6 Ounces Haddock Fillets
- ½ Tablespoon Butter
- ¼ Cup Heavy Cream

**Directions:**

1. Combine your ginger, pepper and salt in a bowl. Rub your fish down this mixture and then set it to the side for fifteen minutes.
2. Press sauté and add in your butter and fish. Cook for two minutes.
3. Pour in the cheese and cream, stirring well.
4. Lock the lid and cook on low pressure for ten minutes.
5. Use a natural pressure release, and then serve topped with the remaining sauce.

# SHRIMP CURRY

**Serves:** 2

**Time:** 15 Minutes

**Calories:** 246

**Protein:** 46 Grams

**Fat:** 2 Grams

**Carbs:** 3 Grams

**Ingredients:**

- 2 Tablespoons Cilantro, Fresh 7 chopped
- 2 Tablespoons Coconut Milk
- 1 lb. Shrimp, Frozen
- ½ Cup Water
- ½ Teaspoon Garam Masala
- 1/8 Teaspoon Cayenne
- ¾ Cup Onion, Chopped
- ½ Teaspoon Sea Salt, Fine

**Directions:**

1. Add all ingredients into your instant pot mini except for your milk and cilantro. Stir all ingredients together.
2. Lock he lid, and then cook on high pressure for five minutes.
3. Use a quick release, and then add in your milk and cilantro.
4. Serve warm.

# SWEET & SOUR FISH

**Serves:** 3

**Time:** 20 Minutes

**Calories:** 402

**Protein:** 22.5 Grams

**Fat:** 23.3 Grams

**Carbs:** 28.1 Grams

**Ingredients:**

- 1 lb. Fish Chunks
- ½ Tablespoon Sugar
- 1 Tablespoon Vinegar
- 1 Tablespoon Olive Oil
- 1 Tablespoon Soy Sauce
- Sea Salt & Black Pepper to Taste

**Directions:**

1. Add in your oil and press sauté.
2. Once your oil is hot add your fish chunks in, and then sauté for three minutes. Add in your remaining ingredients before sealing your instant pot mini.
3. Cook on high pressure for six minutes, and then allow for a natural pressure release before serving warm.

# LEMON DIJON TILAPIA

**Serves:** 2 **Time:** 15 Minutes

**Calories:** 176 **Protein:** 1.2 Grams

**Fat:** 14.4 Grams **Carbs:** 7 Grams

**Ingredients:**

- 2 Large Tilapia Fillets
- 2 Tablespoons Dijon Mustard
- 1 Teaspoon Horseradish, Grated
- ½ Teaspoon Black Pepper
- 1 Tablespoon Lemon Juice, Fresh
- 1 Teaspoon Ginger, Grated Fresh
- 1 Lemon, Sliced
- ½ Teaspoon Sea Salt, Fine
- ½ Tablespoon Olive Oil
- 1 Cup Water

**Directions:**

1. Mix horseradish, Dijon mustard and lemon juice. Season your white fish with salt and pepper before adding it to your Dijon marinade. Allow it to marinate for twenty minutes.

2. Pour your water into your instant pot and then put your steamer rack inside. Place your fillets on the rack before pouring your marinade over top of them.

3. Seal your instant pot and cook on high pressure for four minutes. Allow for a natural pressure release and serve with lemon slices.

# Shrimp & Ricotta Recipe

**Serves:** 3

**Time:** 20 Minutes

**Calories:** 260

**Protein:** 20.4 Grams

**Fat:** 19.7 Grams

**Carbs:** 11.9 Grams

**Ingredients:**

- ½ Teaspoon Cayenne Pepper
- 1 Tablespoon Italian Seasoning, Salt Free
- 2 Tablespoons Butter
- 14.6 Ounces Tomatoes, Canned & Diced
- 2 Cloves Garlic, Mined
- 4 Tablespoons Ricotta Cheese
- ½ lb. Shrimp, Peeled & Deveined
- Sea Salt to taste

**Directions:**

1. Throw your butter into the instant pot and heat it up by pressing sauté. Add in your garlic and cook for a minute. It should become fragrant. Add in your tomatoes, onion, cayenne, salt and Italian seasoning before throwing in your shrimp. Mix well.

2. Seal the lid and cook on high pressure for five minutes.

3. Use a quick release and stir in your ricotta. It's best served warm over noodles.

# Scallop Coconut Curry

**Serves:** 4

**Time:** 25 Minutes

**Calories:** 405

**Protein:** 22.4 Grams

**Fat:** 28.2 Grams

**Carbs:** 12.7 Grams

**Ingredients:**

- 1 Tablespoon Olive Oil
- ½ Teaspoon Sea Salt, Fine
- ½ Teaspoon Nutmeg
- ½ Cup Thai Red Curry Paste
- 1 Teaspoons Soy Sauce
- 1 lb. Scallops
- 1 Cup Coconut Milk
- 1 ½ Cup Chicken Broth
- 1 Teaspoon Curry Powder
- 1 Teaspoon Vinegar

**Directions:**

1. Start by pressing sauté and then add your oil in. once it's hot ad in your scallops. Sauté them for three minutes. Make sure both sides are browned.
2. Add all remaining ingredients and seal. Cook on high pressure for six minutes.
3. Use a quick release and stir. Serve well.

# CHEESY PORK BITES

**Serves:** 2 **Time:** 20 Minutes

**Calories:** 146 **Protein:** 11.2 Grams

**Fat:** 7.9 Grams **Carbs:** 6.2 Grams

**Ingredients:**

- 2 Tablespoons Red Chilies, Chopped
- 2 Tablespoons Milk, Fresh
- 2 Tablespoons Onion, Diced
- ½ lb. Ground Pork
- ¾ Teaspoon Worcestershire Sauce
- 1 Tablespoon Flour
- ¼ Cup Mozzarella Cheese, Cubed
- 1 Egg White
- Sea Salt & Black Pepper to Taste

**Directions:**

1. Start by combining your egg white, pork, milk, flour, onion, salt, pepper and Worcestershire. Mix well, and shape into balls. Each ball should be filled with red chili and mozzarella cubes. Set your balls to the side.

2. Add in your water to your instant pot before adding in your trivet. Arrange your pork balls on your trivet, and then seal your instant pot.

3. Steam for fifteen minutes on high pressure.

4. Allow for a natural pressure release, and then remove the pork balls. Allow them to cool before serving.

# SPICY HONEY CHICKEN

**Serves:** 4

**Time:** 20 Minutes

**Calories:** 155

**Protein:** 17 Grams

**Fat:** 2 Grams

**Carbs:** 15 Grams

## Ingredients:

- 1 Tablespoon Garlic, Minced
- 1 ½ Tablespoons Ginger, Minced
- 1 Tablespoon Brown Sugar
- 2 Tablespoons Cornstarch
- 4 Chicken Breasts
- 3 Tablespoons Honey
- ¼ Cup Soy Sauce
- 1 Teaspoon Worcestershire Sauce
- ½ Onion, Sliced
- 1 Tablespoon Sriracha Sauce
- 2 Green Onions
- 1 Tablespoons Sesame Seeds

## Directions:

1. Start by chopping your chicken breasts into bite sized chunks, and then dice your onion.

2. Add both to your instant pot, and then take a bowl out. In your bowl mix all of your remaining ingredients except for cornstarch. Pour this mixture into the chicken and cover it with the marinade.

3. Close the lid, and cook on high pressure for four minutes.

4. Use a quick release, and then get out another bowl. Add your hot sauce and cornstarch and hot sauce. Whisk it together and place it in your instant pot.

5. Press sauté, and then allow everything to bubble.

6. Allow it to thicken before serving warm.

# CURRY WITH ZUCCHINI

**Serves:** 2 **Time:** 20 Minutes

**Calories:** 243 **Protein:** 33.6 Grams

**Fat:** 8.7 Grams **Carbs:** 5.3 Grams

**Ingredients:**

- 2 Teaspoons Garlic, Minced
- 2 Tablespoons Onion, Chopped
- ¼ Cup Zucchini, Chopped
- ½ lb. Chicken Breast, Boneless
- 1 Teaspoon Curry Powder
- ¼ Teaspoon Brown Sugar
- ½ Cup Water
- ¼ Teaspoon Turmeric
- ¼ Cup Pineapple Chunks
- ¼ Teaspoon Ginger
- Sea Salt & Black Pepper to Taste

**Directions:**

1. Start by chopping your chicken breast and rub it down with garlic, curry powder, ginger, salt, pepper, brown sugar and turmeric. Place this mix into your instant pot.

2. Add in your pineapple chunks and onion before pouring in your water.

3. Cover and seal the lid. Cook for ten minutes on high pressure.

4. Use a natural pressure release, and then add in your zucchini. Stir until it just beings to wilt, and then serve over rice.

# BEEF STEW

**Serves:** 2

**Time:** 1 Hour

**Time:** 570

**Protein:** 53.64 Grams

**Fat:** 26 Grams

**Carbs:** 33.68 Grams

**Ingredients:**

- 2 Tablespoons Butter
- 1 Onion, Chopped
- 2 Tablespoons Flour
- 1 Tablespoon Tomato Paste
- 1 lb. Chuck Beef
- 2 Carrots, Sliced
- 1 Celery Stalk, Sliced
- 1 Teaspoon Thyme
- ½ Teaspoon Rosemary
- ½ Teaspoon Black Pepper
- 2 Cups Beef Broth
- ½ lb. Potatoes, Chopped
- 1 Teaspoon Sea Salt, Fine

**Directions:**

1. Start by sprinkling your beef with salt and pepper before pressing sauté on your instant pot mini. Add in your butter and once it's melted brown your beef. Remove the beef from your instant pot and then put on a plate.

2. Add your celery, carrots and onion, and cook until your onion becomes translucent. Add in your rosemary and thyme, cooking for a half hour. Add in your flour, making sure everything is coated.

3. Add in your beef broth and tomato paste, and make sure that nothing is stuck to the bottom of the pot.

4. Add in your potatoes, and then put your beef in the pot again.

5. Cook for thirty-five minutes on high pressure before using a quick release. Serve warm.

# CHEESY BEEF PIE

**Serves:** 2

**Time:** 20 Minutes

**Calories:** 368

**Protein:** 19.2 Grams

**Fat:** 30.7 Grams

**Carbs:** 3.4 Grams

**Ingredients:**

- ¼ lb. Ground Beef
- 2 Teaspoons Garlic Powder
- ¼ Cup Cheddar Cubes
- 1 Tablespoon Sesame Oil
- 2 Tablespoons Cornstarch
- ½ Teaspoon Black Pepper
- 2 Eggs

**Directions:**

1. Mix all of your ingredients in a pan that fits inside your instant pot mini. Make sure it is evenly spread out, and then pour your water in. add in your trivet. Place your pan on the trivet, and press steam.

2. Cook for fifteen minutes on high pressure. Use a natural pressure release, and allow it to cool before serving.

# WINE CHICKEN PASTA

**Serves:** 4 **Time:** 20 Minutes

**Calories:** 542 **Protein:** 38 Grams

**Fat:** 9 Grams **Carbs:** 63 Grams

**Ingredients:**

- 1 lb. Chicken Breasts, Cubed
- 1 Cup White Wine
- 1 Tablespoon Olive Oil
- 16 Ounces Pasta Sauce
- 3 Cups Water
- 1 Cup Heavy Cream
- 1 Tablespoon Italian Seasoning
- 4 Cloves Garlic, Chopped
- 3 Bell Peppers, Sliced
- **Directions:**

1. Start by sautéing your garlic and onions in oil. Cook them for about a minute so they soften, and then add in your chicken cubes. Cook for another three minutes before adding in your seasoning and white wine. Stir to combine.

2. Add in your pasta with enough water to cover it.

3. Lock the lid, and cook on high pressure for four minutes.

4. Use a quick release, and then press sauté. Stir in your heavy cream, cooking for two more minutes so that it thickens. Mix well and serve warm.

# BEEF LASAGNA

**Serves:** 2

**Time:** 50 Minutes

**Calories:** 712

**Protein:** 56.7 Grams

**Fat:** 19.1 Grams

**Carbs:** 36.1 Grams

## Ingredients:

- 15 Ounces Marinara Sauce
- ½ lb. Ground Beef
- 6 Lasagna Noodles, Uncooked
- 1 Cup Mozzarella Cheese
- 1 Cup Ricotta Cheese
- 1 Tablespoon Olive Oil
- 2 Cups Water
- 2 Cloves Garlic, Minced
- ½ Onion, Chopped
- Sea Salt & Black Pepper to Taste

**Directions:**

1.  Press sauté, and then add in your garlic and onion. Cook for two minutes before adding in your beef. Season with salt and pepper and cook for four additional minutes.

2.  Transfer it all to a plate before adding in your trivet.

3.  Get out a spring form pan, and then place your lasagna pieces on the bottom, adding 1/3 of your sauce, 1/3 of your meat, mozzarella and ricotta. Continue to layer until you run out of ingredients.

4.  Add your water to your instant pot and then place your pan on the trivet.

5.  Close the lid and cook on high pressure for twenty minutes.

6.  Use a natural pressure release, and then turn on the broiler in your oven. Cook for five to six minutes. Your cheese should become browned slightly, and then allow it to cool for about five minutes before slicing.

# Garlic & Spinach Pasta

**Serves:** 3

**Time:** 25 Minutes

**Calories:** 462

**Protein:** 21 Grams

**Fat:** 4 Grams

**Carbs:** 49 Grams

**Ingredients:**

- ½ lbs. Fusilli Pasta, Whole Wheat
- 2 Tablespoons Butter, Cubed
- 2 Cups Spinach, Chopped
- 2 ½ Cups Water
- 1/3 Cup Parmesan, Grated
- Sea Salt & Black Pepper to Taste

**Directions:**

1. Open your lid and then throw in your water and pasta. Add in your garlic and spinach, and stir to combine. Lock the lid and then cook on high pressure for six minutes.

2. Use a quick release, and then season with butter, seasoning and cheese. Combine, and allow it to set for five to ten minutes before serving.

# HERB CHICKEN

**Serves:** 2

**Time:** 25 Minutes

**Calories:** 276

**Protein:** 21.4 Grams

**Fat:** 17.4 Grams

**Carbs:** 6.8 Grams

## Ingredients:

- ¼ Teaspoon Sea Salt, Fine
- ½ Teaspoon Cayenne Pepper
- 2 Red Chilies
- 2 Shallots
- 2 Cloves Garlic
- ½ Cup Water
- ¼ Cup Red Tomatoes, Diced
- 1 Lemon Grass
- 1 Bay Leaf
- ½ lb. Chicken, Bone In
- ½ Teaspoon Turmeric

## Directions:

1. Start by putting the red chilies, cayenne pepper, salt, turmeric, shallots and garlic into a food processor to pulse until smooth.

2. Transfer this spice mixture into a bowl and add in your red tomatoes, and mix well.

3. Cut the chicken into medium pieces and rub it down with the spice mixture.

4. Put it on a sheet of aluminum foil with lemongrass and your bay leaf on top and then wrap it up.

5. Pour your water into the instant pot mini, placing your trivet inside.

6. Your foil wrapped chicken will be placed on top for that trivet. Seal the lid.

7. Cook on high pressure for twelve minutes, and then use a natural pressure release.

8. Take the wrapped chicken out and unwrap it to serve warm. It goes best with rice.

# Honey Chicken

**Serves:** 3

**Time:** 35 Minutes

**Calories:** 544

**Protein:** 36.2 Grams

**Fat:** 22 Grams

**Carbs:** 48.2 Grams

**Ingredients:**

- 2 lb. Chicken Thighs, Boneless
- ¼ Cup Ghee
- ¼ Cup Honey, Raw
- 3 Tablespoons Tamari
- 3 Tablespoons Ketchup
- 2 Teaspoons Garlic Powder
- ½ Teaspoon Black Pepper
- 1 ½ Teaspoons Sea Salt, Fine

**Directions:**

1. Start by adding all of your ingredients into the pot, and then seal the lid.
2. Cook on high pressure for eighteen minutes, and then allow for a natural pressure release.
3. Serve warm. It goes great with vegetables and rice.

# CALIFORNIA CHICKEN

**Serves:** 3 **Time:** 25 Minutes

**Calories:** 192 **Protein:** 14.4 Grams

**Fat:** 27.7 Grams **Carbs:** 1.9 Grams

**Ingredients:**

- 3 Chicken Breast Halves, Boneless & Skinless
- ½ Lemon, Sliced Thin
- ½ Cup White Wine
- ¼ Cup Parsley, Chopped
- 2 Tablespoons Olive Oil
- 1 Cup Chicken Broth
- 1 Teaspoon Rosemary
- Sea Salt & Black Pepper to Taste
- 2 Cloves Garlic, Peeled & Sliced

**Directions:**

1. Press sauté and add in your oil.
2. Add your chicken breast sin and cook for about seven minutes per side so that all sides are browned.
3. Season with garlic and rosemary, and then add in your broth, parsley and wine.
4. Close the lid and cook on high pressure for eight minutes.
5. Use a quick release and serve with lemon slices.

# Shredded Chicken with Sauce

**Serves:** 2 **Time:** 20 Minutes

**Calories:** 352 **Protein:** 26.1 Grams

**Fat:** 24.7 Grams

**Carbs:** 7.8 Grams

**Ingredients:**

- ½ Teaspoon Cumin
- ½ lb. Chicken Breast, Boneless
- 2 Tablespoons chicken Broth
- ¼ Cup Orange Juice, Fresh
- ½ Teaspoon Orange Zest, Grated
- 3 Teaspoons Garlic, Minced
- 2 Tablespoons Onion, Chopped
- 1 Bay Leaf
- 2 Tablespoons Mayonnaise
- 1 Tablespoon Tomato Chili Sauce
- ¼ Teaspoon Chili Powder
- ¼ Teaspoon Oregano
- ¼ Teaspoon Sea Salt, Fine
- ¼ Teaspoon Black Pepper

## Directions:

1. Start by putting your chicken in the instant pot min, seasoning it with chili powder, cumin, oregano, salt, pepper, minced garlic, orange zest and onion. Add your bay leaf before pouring in your orange juice and chicken broth.

2. Seal the lid, and then cook on your chicken setting which is high pressure for twelve minutes.

3. While this is cooking combine your mayonnaise, slat, garlic, and tomato. Stir well and place it to the side.

4. Allow for a natural pressure release when the chicken is done, and then take your chicken out. Leave your liquid in the instant pot. Use a fork in order to shred your chicken before turning it to your instant pot mini, and stir it well so that it's completely coated with the juices.

5. Transfer the now coated and shredded chicken to a plate before drizzling it with your mayonnaise sauce to serve.

# GREEK TURKEY

**Serves:** 3

**Time:** 10 Minutes

**Calories:** 932

**Protein:** 84.7 Grams

**Fat:** 32.2 Grams

**Carbs:** 15.7 Grams

**Ingredients:**

- 1 Turkey Breast, Sliced
- ½ Poblano Pepper, Minced
- ½ Teaspoon Chili Flakes
- 3 Tablespoons Olives, Sliced
- ½ Cup Tomatoes, diced
- ½ Cup Feta Cheese, Crumbled
- 2 Tablespoons Lemon Juice
- 1 Cup Water
- 2 Tablespoons Olive Oil
- 3 Cloves Garlic, Minced
- ½ Teaspoon Rosemary
- ½ Teaspoon Basil
- Chopped Parsley
- Sea Salt & Black Pepper to Taste

**Directions:**

1. Get out a large bowl and place your garlic, lemon juice, poblano pepper, olive oil, salt, chili flakes, basil, rosemary and pepper in it.

2. Mix all ingredients well, and then marinate your turkey in it. Cover it with plastic wrap before placing it in the fridge for up to three hours.

3. Pour water into your instant pot, and then put a trivet in it. Place your turkey pieces on your trivet. Pour your marinade over it generously, and then cook on high pressure for fifty minutes.

4. Use a quick release, and top with tomato slice, cheese and olives. Grill for ten minutes or place in the oven for ten minutes before serving with fresh parsley.

# Snacks & Side Dish Recipes

## Parmesan Potatoes

**Serves:** 2 **Time:** 10 Minutes

**Calories:** 343 **Protein:** 16 Grams

**Fat:** 2 Grams **Carbs:** 24 Grams

**Ingredients:**

- 3 Tablespoons Butter
- 1 Cup Water
- 2 Tablespoons Parsley, Chopped
- ½ Cup Milk
- 3 Potatoes, Peeled & Cubed
- ¼ Cup Parmesan Cheese, Grated
- 1 Teaspoon Sea Salt, Fine
- ¼ Teaspoon Black Pepper

**Directions:**

1. Throw your potatoes in with a cup of water, and then stir. Lock the lid, and cook for three minutes on high pressure. Use a quick release, and then drain your potatoes.
2. Add in your remaining ingredients except for parmesan and parsley.
3. Serve topped with parmesan and parsley while still warm.

# KALE & CASHEW DELIGHT

**Serves:** 2

**Time:** 10 Minutes

**Calories:** 286

**Protein:** 17 Grams

**Fat:** 4 Grams

**Carbs:** 26 Grams

**Ingredients:**

- ½ Cup Cashews, Raw
- ¼ Cup Nutritional Yeast
- 1 Cup Water
- 5 Ounces Kale
- 1 Teaspoon Vinegar
- ½ Tablespoon Seasoning of Your Choice

**Directions:**

1. Start by placing your water and kale in the instant pot and lock it. Cook on high pressure for four minutes.

2. Use a quick release, and then puree your cashews, seasonings and yeast in a food processor.

3. Transfer your kale to a serving plate and toss with seasoning.

# EASY BLACK BEANS

**Serves:** 4 **Time:** 45 Minutes

**Calories:** 232

**Protein:** 13.3 Grams

**Fat:** 0.8 Grams

**Carbs:** 35.7 Grams

**Ingredients:**

- 1 Cup Black Beans, dry
- ½ Onion, Diced
- 3 Cups Vegetable Broth
- ¼ Teaspoon Sea Salt, Fine
- 1 ½ Teaspoon Oregano
- ½ Teaspoon Coriander Powder
- 3 Cloves Garlic, Minced
- ½ Teaspoon Smoked Paprika
- 2 Teaspoons Cumin
- 1 Teaspoon Chili Powder
- 1 Bay Leaf
- Chopped Mixed Vegetables
- Cilantro for Serving
- Cheese for serving
- Sour Cream for Serving

**Directions:**

1. Press sauté and then add in your oil. Add in your vegetables and stir. Cook until they're almost done before adding in your onion. Stir occasionally so it doesn't burn.

2. Add in your garlic, bay leaf, oregano, cumin, paprika, pepper, salt, coriander, and chili powder. Add in your garlic, and stir frequently so it doesn't burn.

3. Add in your broth and beans, and make sure to continue stirring. Seal your instant pot and then cook on high pressure for thirty-five minus.

4. Allow for a natural pressure release, and then then garnish before serving.

# WALNUT & BEET BOWL

**Serves:** 3 **Time:** 10 Minutes

**Calories:** 151 **Protein:** 2.7 Grams

**Fat:** 10 Grams

**Carbs:** 15.2 Grams

**Ingredients:**

- 1 ½ lb. Beets, Scrubbed & Rinsed
- 2 Teaspoons Lemon Juice
- 1 Teaspoon Dijon Mustard
- 2 Teaspoons Apple Cider Vinegar
- 1 ½ Tablespoons Olive Oil
- 2 Tablespoons Walnuts, Chopped
- 1 ½ Teaspoons Sugar
- 2 Cups Water
- Sea Salt & Black Pepper to Taste

**Directions:**

1. Pour in your water and add in your beets. Lock the lid and cook for ten minutes on high pressure.
2. Turn the pot off, and allow for a natural release.
3. Open the lids and transfer your beets to a bowl. Chop them to bite sized pieces and all remaining ingredients except for oil and walnuts.
4. Whisk to combine and then add in your walnuts and oil right before serving.

# CHEESY ASPARAGUS

**Serves:** 4

**Time:** 10 Minutes

**Calories:** 265

**Protein:** 4.6 Grams

**Fat:** 26.6 Grams

**Carbs:** 2.6 Grams

**Ingredients:**

- 1 Handful Asparagus
- ¼ Cup Butter
- 3 Tablespoons Cheddar Cheese, Grated
- 3 Teaspoons Garlic, Minced

**Directions:**

1. Start by trimming the asparagus, and then get out an aluminum pan that's disposable. Sprinkle your garlic over your asparagus in your pan.
2. Drop your butter on top of your asparagus in several different places. Pour in your water and then add in your trivet with your pan on top.
3. Cook for four minutes on steam.
4. Allow for a natural pressure release and serve warm.

# GREEN BEAN STIR FRY

**Serves:** 4

**Time:** 10 Minutes

**Calories:** 85

**Protein:** 2.4 Grams

**Fat:** 5.4 Grams

**Carbs:** 9.1 Grams

**Ingredients:**

- ½ lb. Green Beans, Chopped
- ¾ Tablespoon Olive Oil
- 2 Teaspoons Garlic, Minced
- 1 Teaspoon Fish Sauce
- ¼ Teaspoon Sea Salt, Fine

**Directions:**

1. Pour your water in and then add in your trivet.
2. Place your green beans on the trivet, and then seal your instant pot.
3. Cook your green beans on low pressure two minutes.
4. Use a quick release, and then remove them from the instant pot. Wipe your instant pot out, and then add in your olive oil. Add in your garlic and sauté for a minute.
5. Add in your green beans and season with salt and fish sauce. Stir well and cook for another minute before serving.

# GLAZED CARROTS

**Serves:** 4

**Time:** 8 Minutes

**Calories:** 50

**Protein:** 3.9 Grams

**Fat:** 0.4 Grams

**Carbs:** 10.5 Grams

**Ingredients:**

- ¼ lb. Carrots
- ½ Tablespoon Butter
- 1 Tablespoon Honey
- ¼ Cup Vegetable Broth
- ½ Teaspoon Cinnamon
- ¼ Teaspoon Sea Salt, Fine

**Directions:**

1. Peel your carrots before setting them aside.
2. Pour the vegetable broth into your instant pot before adding in the trivet and rub the carrots down with salt. Place the salted carrots on the trivet, and then cook on high pressure for two minutes.
3. Use a natural pressure release, and then plate your carrots.
4. Clean your instant pot out and then add in the butter. Return your carrots to the instant pot and sprinkle with cinnamon and a honey drizzle. Press sauté and cook for one minute more before serving.

# SPICY CABBAGE

**Serves:** 4

**Time:** 10 Minutes

**Calories:** 70

**Protein:** 2.3 Grams

**Fat:** 2.5 Grams

**Carbs:** 11.6 Grams

**Ingredients:**

- ¾ lb. Cabbage
- ½ Cup Water
- ½ Teaspoon Sugar
- ¼ Cup Carrots, Grated
- ½ Teaspoon Cayenne Pepper
- 1 Teaspoon Sesame Oil

**Directions:**

1. Slice your cabbage into wedges before placing them to the side. Add your sesame oil to the instant pot, and then press sauté.
2. Add in your cabbage wedges and cook for three minutes.
3. Sprinkle in your sugar, grated carrots, and cayenne pepper.
4. Pour your water into the instant pot and then seal it.
5. Cook on high pressure for five minutes.
6. Use a natural release, and then serve warm.

# Easy Asparagus

**Serves:** 2

**Time:** 10 Minutes

**Calories:** 86

**Protein:** 3 Grams

**Fat:** 2 Grams

**Carbs:** 5 Grams

**Ingredients:**

- 1 Tablespoon Olive Oil
- ½ Tablespoon Onion, Diced
- ½ lb. Asparagus Spears, Trimmed
- 1 Cup Water
- 1/8 Teaspoon Garlic Powder
- Sea Salt to Taste

**Directions:**

1. Pour your water into the pot and then place a trivet inside. Add your asparagus on top before drizzling your oil over it. Sprinkle with onions, garlic and salt.
2. Pres steam, and cook on high pressure for two minutes.
3. Use a quick release, and serve warm.

# PEA & POTATO SIDE

**Serves:** 2 **Time:** 35 Minutes

**Calories:** 312 **Protein:** 11 Grams

**Fat:** 8 Grams **Carbs:** 34 Grams

**Ingredients:**

- 2 Cups Vegetable Stock
- 1 Tablespoon Butter
- 1 Potato, Chopped
- 1 Clove Garlic, Crushed
- 1 Cup Yellow Peas, Split
- ½ Cup Onions, Chopped
- ½ Teaspoon Cayenne Pepper
- ½ Carrot, Sliced Thin
- Sea Salt to Taste

**Directions:**

1. Start by pressing sauté and cook your onions and butter. Allow them to cook for two minutes so that your onion softens.
2. Add in your vegetables, and fry for about six minutes. Season with cayenne and salt, cooking for another sixty seconds.
3. Add in your vegetable stock, and stir well.
4. Lock the lid and cook on high pressure for twenty-five minutes.
5. Use a quick release, and then serve warm.

# Dessert Recipes

## Tapioca Pudding

**Serves:** 2 **Time:** 18 Minutes

**Calories:** 214 **Protein:** 5.1 Grams

**Fat:** 3.2 Grams

**Carbs:** 41.8 Grams

**Ingredients:**

- 1 ¼ Cup Milk
- 1 ½ Cup Water
- ½ Teaspoon Stevia Sweetener
- ½ Lemon, Sliced
- 1 Tablespoon Lemon Zest
- ½ Cup Tapioca Pearls, Rinsed & Drained

**Directions:**

1. Pour in a cup of water and then get out a baking dish. In that baking dish mix, all of your ingredients. Make sure your sweetener dissolves. Place your trivet in, and put the pan on the trivet.

2. Cook on high pressure for six minutes.

3. Allow for a quick release, and then serve with lemon wedges. It can be served warm or chilled.

# PINEAPPLE PUDDING

**Serves:** 3

**Time:** 20 Minutes

**Calories:** 386

**Protein:** 15 Grams

**Fat:** 2 Grams

**Carbs:** 21 Grams

**Ingredients:**

- 1 Cup Maple Syrup
- 2/3 Cup Pineapples, Crushed
- 1 Can Coconut Milk
- 1 Cup Arborio Rice
- 1 ½ Cups Water
- 1 Tablespoon Cinnamon

**Directions:**

1. Start by opening the lid and adding your rice and water. Stir well and then ad in all remaining ingredients. Stir again until well combined

2. Cook on low pressure for twelve minutes.

3. Use a quick release, and then open the lid.

4. Add in half of your coconut milk, maple syrup, cinnamon and pineapple. Stir well to combine, and then mix in the remaining milk.

5. Serve warm or chilled.

# HONEY PANNA COTTA

**Serves:** 2 **Time:** 30 Minutes

**Calories;** 343 **Protein:** 5.08 Grams

**Fat:** 4.1 Grams **Carbs:** 75.25 Grams

**Ingredients:**

- 1 Cup Yogurt, Plain
- 1 Teaspoon Vanilla Extract, Pure
- 1 Tablespoon Hot water
- ¼ Cup Sugar
- 1 Orange, Juiced
- 1 Teaspoon Gelatin, Unflavored
- ¼ Cup Honey, Raw
- ¼ Teaspoon Cardamom

**Directions:**

1. Whisk your sugar, yogurt and vanilla together and put it to the side.
2. Sprinkle your gelatin in the water and allow it to soften. Whisk until it completely dissolves. Add this into your yogurt mixture, and then get out two small ramekins. Chill for two hours, and while its chills make your sauce.
3. To make your sauce combine your orange, cardamom and honey in your instant pot, and then close the lid. Cook for one minute, and then chill it completely.
4. Once your panna cotta is set, run a knife around your ramekin and invert it so that it plates. Drizzle with sauce.

# EASY BANANA BREAD

**Serves:** 4

**Time:** 40 Minutes

**Calories:** 267

**Protein:** 13.7 Grams

**Fat:** 20.4 Grams

**Carbs:** 6.6 Grams

## Ingredients:

- 2 Cups Water
- Pinch Sea Salt
- 1 Egg
- ½ Teaspoon Baking Powder
- 1 Teaspoon Baking Soda
- 1/3 Cup Milk
- 2 Cups Four
- 1/3 Cup Butter
- ¾ Cup Sugar
- 2 Bananas, Mashed
- 3 Teaspoons Lemon Juice

**Directions:**

1. Mix your lemon and milk together in a butter. Add in your sugar, egg and mashed bananas, making sure it's well combined.

2. Get out a separate bowl and mix your baking soda, baking powder and flour with a pinch of salt.

3. Add your ghee to the mixture, and mix constantly.

4. Add this to your milk mixture, and then grease a cake pan that fits in your instant pot. Cover with foil and make sure it's sealed tight.

5. Add in your water, and then add a trivet into your Instant pot.

6. Place your pan on the trivet, and seal the lid.

7. Cook on high pressure for thirty minutes.

8. Allow for a natural pressure release, and allow it to cool before slicing.

# PUMPKIN PIE

**Serves:** 3

**Time:** 45 Minutes

**Calories:** 413

**Protein:** 6.1 Grams

**Fat:** 13.85 Grams

**Carbs:** 68.5 Grams

**Ingredients:**

- 1 Can Pumpkin
- ½ Cup Milk
- ½ Teaspoon Nutmeg
- 1 Graham Cracker Pie Crust in Aluminum Pan
- ½ Cup Milk
- 1 Teaspoon Cinnamon
- 1 Egg

**Directions:**

1. Blend your egg, milk, pumpkin, sugar, cinnamon and nutmeg. Pour it into your crust.
2. Add in your water and trivet, and then put the pie on top.
3. Close and cook on high pressure for thirty-five minutes.

# BERRY CHEESECAKE

**Serves:** 4

**Time:** 30 Minutes

**Calories:** 254

**Protein:** 16.7 Grams

**Fat:** 23.9 Grams

**Carbs:** 3.7 Grams

## Ingredients:

- ½ Cup Strawberries, Chopped
- ½ Cup Blackberries
- 1 Teaspoons Vanilla Extract, Pure
- 6 Tablespoons Sugar
- 2 Eggs
- 1 Teaspoon Butter
- 1 ½ Packs 8 Ounce Cream Cheese / 1 Cup Water

## Directions:

1. Start by getting out a spring form pan and greasing it with butter. Make sure that the pan fits into your instant pot, and then blend your cream cheese together until smooth.

2. Add in your vanilla extract and sugar, mixing well.

3. Add in your eggs one at a time, mixing until they're well incorporated.

4. Add in your blackberries and strawberries to the batter, making sure it's well mixed.

5. Pour in the cheesecake batter into the pan, and then wrap it with foil tightly.

6. Place a trivet into your instant pot, pouring your water in. add your pan on top of the trivet.

7. Cook on high pressure for twenty minutes, and then allow for a natural pressure release.

8. Refrigerate for an hour before topping with mix berries.

# RAISIN APPLES

**Serves:** 2

**Time:** 15 Minutes

**Calories:** 377

**Protein:** 3.5 Grams

**Fat:** 0 Grams

**Carbs:** 62 Grams

**Ingredients:**

- 2 Apples, Cored
- 3 Tablespoons Raisins
- ¼ Cup Sugar
- ½ Teaspoon Cinnamon
- ¼ Cup Red Wine

**Directions:**

1. Start by placing all ingredients in your instant pot and close the lid.
2. Cook on high pressure for ten minutes.
3. Use a natural pressure release before serving warm.

# RICOTTA APPLE CAKE

**Serves:** 2 **Time:** 25 Minutes

**Calories:** 431 **Protein:** 13 Grams

**Fat:** 4 Grams **Carbs:** 57 Grams

**Ingredients:**

- 1 Egg \ 1 Red Apple, Diced
- 1/8 Cup Sugar
- 1 ½ Tablespoons Oil\ ½ Cup Ricotta
- ½ Cup Whole Wheat flour
- 1 Green Apple, Sliced
- ½ Teaspoons Vanilla Extract, Pure
- ½ Teaspoon Baking Soda
- 1 Teaspoon Baking Powder
- ½ Teaspoon Lemon Juice

**Directions:**

1.  Get out a baking sheet that fits inside of your instant pot mini, and then line it with parchment paper. Add in all of your apple slices to the bottom, drizzling the lemon juice over them.

2.  Get out a bowl and whisk all remaining ingredients, including your diced apple. Add your batter over the apples, and then pour two cups of water into your instant pot. Add your trivet with the pan on top.

3.  Lock the lid, and cook for twenty minutes on high pressure. Use a quick release, and then slice and enjoy.

# WINE PEARS

**Serves:** 2

**Time:** 20 Minutes

**Calories:** 328

**Protein:** 2 Grams

**Fat:** 3 Grams

**Carbs:** 38.5 Grams

**Ingredients:**

- 1 Clove
- ½ Cup Sugar
- 2 Pears, Peeled
- 1 Piece Ginger
- 1 Cinnamon Stick
- ¼ Bottle Red Wine of Your choice

**Directions:**

1. Start by adding all of your ingredients into the instant pot, and then close the lid.
2. Cook on high pressure for six minutes, and then use a quick release.
3. Switch the pot to sauté, and allow the liquid to reduce by half. Serve it with the hot juices over it.

# EASY BROWNIES

**Serves:** 2 **Time:** 30 Minutes

**Calories:** 524 **Protein:** 6.45 Grams

**Fat:** 26.25 Grams **Carbs:** 70.72 Grams

**Ingredients:**

- 2/3 Cup Flour
- 1 Cup Sugar
- 2 Eggs
- 1 Teaspoon Vanilla
- 1/3 Cup Cocoa Powder
- ½ Teaspoon Baking Powder
- ½ Cup Butter
- ½ Teaspoon Sea Salt, Fine

**Directions:**

1. Cream your butter with your sugar and beat in each egg one at a time. Add in the vanilla, and then take out a separate bowl. Whisk your flour, cocoa, salt and baking powder.
2. Fold your dry ingredients into the wet ones, and pour this batter into the pan.
3. Place your water in your instant pot followed by the trivet with the pan on top.
4. Seal the lid and cook on high pressure for twenty minutes. Use a quick release and serve room temperature or warm.

# CHOCOLATE CAKE RAMEKINS

**Serves:** 2 **Time:** 20 Minutes

**Calories:** 561 **Protein:** 7 Grams

**Fat:** 32.5 Grams **Carbs:** 58 Grams

**Ingredients:**

- ¼ Cup Butter / ½ Cup Confectioner's sugar
- ½ Teaspoon Vanilla Extract, Pure
- ½ Teaspoon Instant Coffee
- 1 Egg / 1 Egg Yolk
- 2 Ounces Semi-Sweet Chocolate, Chopped
- 3 Tablespoons All Purpose Flour
- ½ Tablespoon Sugar
- 1/8 Teaspoon Sea Salt, Fine

**Directions:**

1. Start by greasing two ramekins and coat them with sugar.
2. Get out a mixing bowl and combine your butter and chocolate with your confectioner's sugar. Make sure it's well combined.
3. Whisk your vanilla, coffee, egg yolk and egg in, and add in your salt and flour. Make sure it's well combined before dividing between ramekins.
4. Pour in two cups of water and then put your trivet in with the ramekins on top.
5. Close the pot and seal the lid.
6. Cook on high pressure for nine minutes and then use a quick release.
7. Top with powdered sugar before serving.

# Pumpkin Cake

**Serves:** 4 **Time:** 45 Minutes

**Calories:** 237 **Protein:** 15.2 Grams

**Fat:** 18.9 Grams

**Carbs:** 28.9 Grams

**Ingredients:**

- 2 Cups Pumpkin Puree
- 2 Tablespoons Pumpkin Pie Spice
- ½ Cup Honey
- 1 Cup Water
- 3 Eggs
- ½ Cup Milk
- Pinch Sea Salt

**Directions:**

1. Start by getting out a bowl and mixing your puree with your eggs. You may also want to use a blender. Add in your honey, spice and milk. Add in your salt and mix again.

2. Grease a round cake pan that's six inches, and then spray it with a coconut oil base. Pour in the cake batter before covering the pan with foil. Make sure it's covered tightly. Pour the water into your instant pot before adding in the trivet.

3. Put your pan on the trivet and cook for thirty-five minutes on high pressure and then use a natural pressure release.

4. Allow it to cool before serving.

# Conclusion

Now you know everything that you need to start cooking with your instant pot mini so that you can eat healthy and delicious recipes without slaving over the kitchen. With a miniature instant pot, your cooking time has been cut in half, and there's no need to sacrifice flavor. Just pick a recipe to get started, and remember that you can use this cookware any time during the day. From breakfast to dessert, there's a little something for everyone. Make it easier to cook for yourself or even for your family with a miniature instant pot that's sure to bake up tasty, easy food.

Made in the USA
Middletown, DE
27 December 2019